PYROGRAPHY PATTERNS

PYROGRAPHY WOODBURNING DESIGNS AND PATTERNS

MW00872557

_____

_____

_____

Settings

Pyrography

Material:	
Tool burning tip:	
Temperature:	
Shading - 1 firing tip:	
Temperature:	
Shading - 2 firing tip:	
Temperature:	
Shading - 3 firing tip:	
Temperature:	

Settings

Pyrography

Material:	
Tool burning tip:	
Temperature:	
Shading - 1 firing tip:	
Temperature:	
Shading - 2 firing tip:	
Temperature:	
Shading - 3 firing tip:	
Temperature:	

Settings

Pyrography

Material:	
Tool burning tip:	
Temperature:	
Shading - 1 firing tip:	
Temperature:	
Shading - 2 firing tip:	
Temperature:	
Shading - 3 firing tip:	
Temperature:	

Settings

Pyrography

Material:	
Tool burning tip:	
Temperature:	
Shading - 1 firing tip:	
Temperature:	
Shading - 2 firing tip:	
Temperature:	
Shading - 3 firing tip:	
Temperature:	

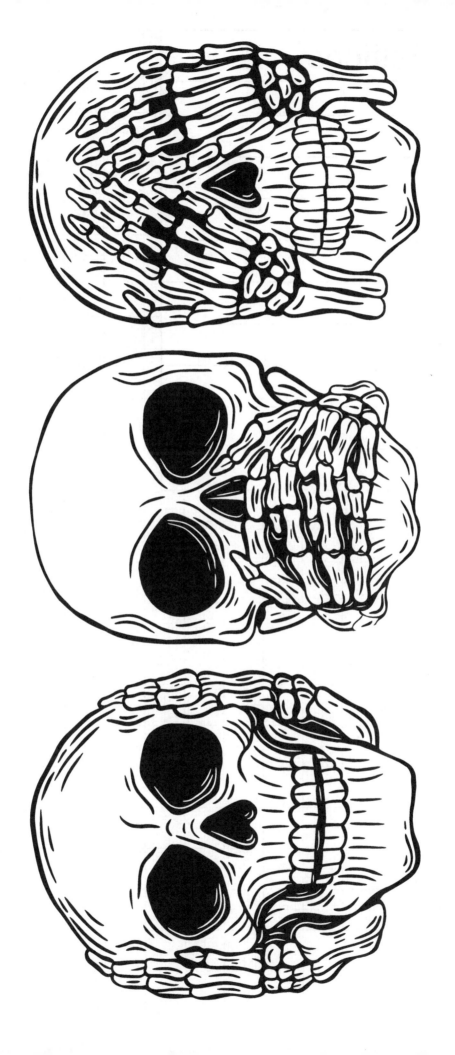

Settings

Pyrography

Material:	
Tool burning tip:	
Temperature:	
Shading - 1 firing tip:	
Temperature:	
Shading - 2 firing tip:	
Temperature:	
Shading - 3 firing tip:	
Temperature:	

Settings

Pyrography

Material:	
Tool burning tip:	
Temperature:	
Shading - 1 firing tip:	
Temperature:	
Shading - 2 firing tip:	
Temperature:	
Shading - 3 firing tip:	
Temperature:	

Settings

Pyrography

Material:	
Tool burning tip:	
Temperature:	
Shading - 1 firing tip:	
Temperature:	
Shading - 2 firing tip:	
Temperature:	
Shading - 3 firing tip:	
Temperature:	

Settings

Settings

Pyrography

Material:	
Tool burning tip:	
Temperature:	
Shading - 1 firing tip:	
Temperature:	
Shading - 2 firing tip:	
Temperature:	
Shading - 3 firing tip:	
Temperature:	

Settings

Pyrography

Material:	
Tool burning tip:	
Temperature:	
Shading - 1 firing tip:	
Temperature:	
Shading - 2 firing tip:	
Temperature:	
Shading - 3 firing tip:	
Temperature:	

Settings

Pyrography

Material:	
Tool burning tip:	
Temperature:	
Shading - 1 firing tip:	
Temperature:	
Shading - 2 firing tip:	
Temperature:	
Shading - 3 firing tip:	
Temperature:	

Settings

Pyrography

Material:	
Tool burning tip:	
Temperature:	
Shading - 1 firing tip:	
Temperature:	
Shading - 2 firing tip:	
Temperature:	
Shading - 3 firing tip:	
Temperature:	

Settings

Settings

Pyrography

Material:	
Tool burning tip:	
Temperature:	
Shading - 1 firing tip:	
Temperature:	
Shading - 2 firing tip:	
Temperature:	
Shading - 3 firing tip:	
Temperature:	

Settings

Pyrography

Material:	
Tool burning tip:	
Temperature:	
Shading - 1 firing tip:	
Temperature:	
Shading - 2 firing tip:	
Temperature:	
Shading - 3 firing tip:	
Temperature:	

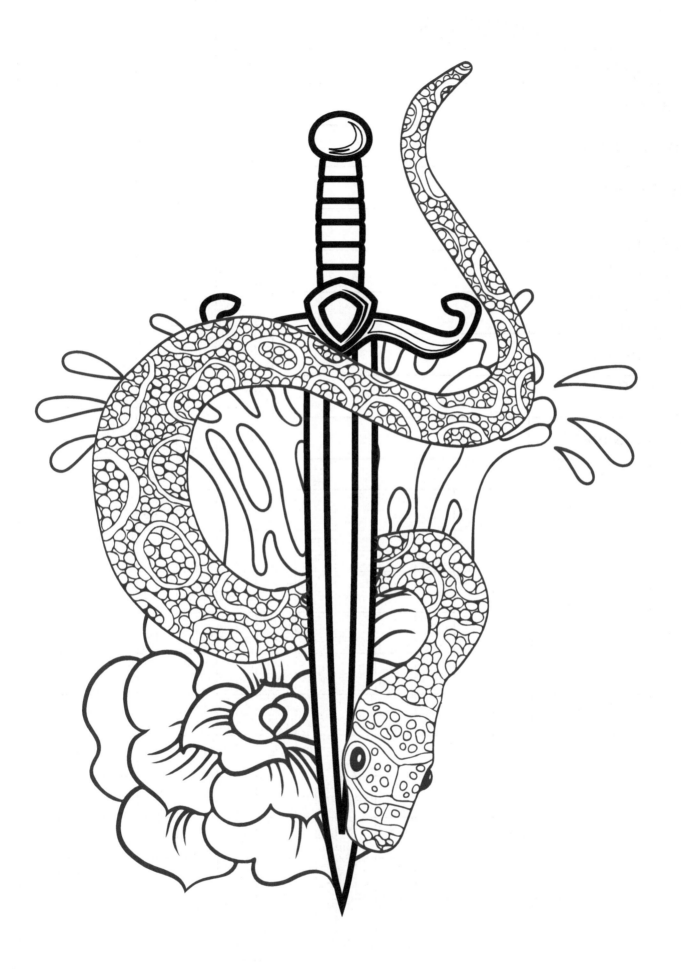

Settings

Pyrography

Material:	
Tool burning tip:	
Temperature:	
Shading - 1 firing tip:	
Temperature:	
Shading - 2 firing tip:	
Temperature:	
Shading - 3 firing tip:	
Temperature:	

Settings

Pyrography

Material:	
Tool burning tip:	
Temperature:	
Shading - 1 firing tip:	
Temperature:	
Shading - 2 firing tip:	
Temperature:	
Shading - 3 firing tip:	
Temperature:	

Settings

Pyrography

Material:	
Tool burning tip:	
Temperature:	
Shading - 1 firing tip:	
Temperature:	
Shading - 2 firing tip:	
Temperature:	
Shading - 3 firing tip:	
Temperature:	

Settings

Pyrography

Material:	
Tool burning tip:	
Temperature:	
Shading - 1 firing tip:	
Temperature:	
Shading - 2 firing tip:	
Temperature:	
Shading - 3 firing tip:	
Temperature:	

Settings

Pyrography

Material:	
Tool burning tip:	
Temperature:	
Shading - 1 firing tip:	
Temperature:	
Shading - 2 firing tip:	
Temperature:	
Shading - 3 firing tip:	
Temperature:	

Settings

Pyrography

Material:	
Tool burning tip:	
Temperature:	
Shading - 1 firing tip:	
Temperature:	
Shading - 2 firing tip:	
Temperature:	
Shading - 3 firing tip:	
Temperature:	

Settings

Pyrography

Material:	
Tool burning tip:	
Temperature:	
Shading - 1 firing tip:	
Temperature:	
Shading - 2 firing tip:	
Temperature:	
Shading - 3 firing tip:	
Temperature:	

Settings

Pyrography

Material:	
Tool burning tip:	
Temperature:	
Shading - 1 firing tip:	
Temperature:	
Shading - 2 firing tip:	
Temperature:	
Shading - 3 firing tip:	
Temperature:	

Settings

Pyrography

Material:	
Tool burning tip:	
Temperature:	
Shading - 1 firing tip:	
Temperature:	
Shading - 2 firing tip:	
Temperature:	
Shading - 3 firing tip:	
Temperature:	

Settings

Pyrography

Material:	
Tool burning tip:	
Temperature:	
Shading - 1 firing tip:	
Temperature:	
Shading - 2 firing tip:	
Temperature:	
Shading - 3 firing tip:	
Temperature:	

Settings

Pyrography

Material:	
Tool burning tip:	
Temperature:	
Shading - 1 firing tip:	
Temperature:	
Shading - 2 firing tip:	
Temperature:	
Shading - 3 firing tip:	
Temperature:	

Settings

Pyrography

Material:	
Tool burning tip:	
Temperature:	
Shading - 1 firing tip:	
Temperature:	
Shading - 2 firing tip:	
Temperature:	
Shading - 3 firing tip:	
Temperature:	

Settings

Pyrography

Material:	
Tool burning tip:	
Temperature:	
Shading - 1 firing tip:	
Temperature:	
Shading - 2 firing tip:	
Temperature:	
Shading - 3 firing tip:	
Temperature:	

Settings

Pyrography

Material:	
Tool burning tip:	
Temperature:	
Shading - 1 firing tip:	
Temperature:	
Shading - 2 firing tip:	
Temperature:	
Shading - 3 firing tip:	
Temperature:	

Settings

Pyrography

Material:	
Tool burning tip:	
Temperature:	
Shading - 1 firing tip:	
Temperature:	
Shading - 2 firing tip:	
Temperature:	
Shading - 3 firing tip:	
Temperature:	

Settings

Pyrography

Material:	
Tool burning tip:	
Temperature:	
Shading - 1 firing tip:	
Temperature:	
Shading - 2 firing tip:	
Temperature:	
Shading - 3 firing tip:	
Temperature:	

Settings

Pyrography

Material:	
Tool burning tip:	
Temperature:	
Shading - 1 firing tip:	
Temperature:	
Shading - 2 firing tip:	
Temperature:	
Shading - 3 firing tip:	
Temperature:	

Settings

Pyrography

Material:	
Tool burning tip:	
Temperature:	
Shading - 1 firing tip:	
Temperature:	
Shading - 2 firing tip:	
Temperature:	
Shading - 3 firing tip:	
Temperature:	

Settings

Pyrography

Material:	
Tool burning tip:	
Temperature:	
Shading - 1 firing tip:	
Temperature:	
Shading - 2 firing tip:	
Temperature:	
Shading - 3 firing tip:	
Temperature:	

Settings

Pyrography

Material:	
Tool burning tip:	
Temperature:	
Shading - 1 firing tip:	
Temperature:	
Shading - 2 firing tip:	
Temperature:	
Shading - 3 firing tip:	
Temperature:	

Settings

Settings

Pyrography

Material:	
Tool burning tip:	
Temperature:	
Shading - 1 firing tip:	
Temperature:	
Shading - 2 firing tip:	
Temperature:	
Shading - 3 firing tip:	
Temperature:	

Settings

Pyrography

Material:	
Tool burning tip:	
Temperature:	
Shading - 1 firing tip:	
Temperature:	
Shading - 2 firing tip:	
Temperature:	
Shading - 3 firing tip:	
Temperature:	

Settings

Pyrography

Material:	
Tool burning tip:	
Temperature:	
Shading - 1 firing tip:	
Temperature:	
Shading - 2 firing tip:	
Temperature:	
Shading - 3 firing tip:	
Temperature:	

Settings

Pyrography

Material:	
Tool burning tip:	
Temperature:	
Shading - 1 firing tip:	
Temperature:	
Shading - 2 firing tip:	
Temperature:	
Shading - 3 firing tip:	
Temperature:	

Settings

Pyrography

Material:	
Tool burning tip:	
Temperature:	
Shading - 1 firing tip:	
Temperature:	
Shading - 2 firing tip:	
Temperature:	
Shading - 3 firing tip:	
Temperature:	

Settings

Pyrography

Material:	
Tool burning tip:	
Temperature:	
Shading - 1 firing tip:	
Temperature:	
Shading - 2 firing tip:	
Temperature:	
Shading - 3 firing tip:	
Temperature:	

Settings

Pyrography

Material:	
Tool burning tip:	
Temperature:	
Shading - 1 firing tip:	
Temperature:	
Shading - 2 firing tip:	
Temperature:	
Shading - 3 firing tip:	
Temperature:	

Settings

Pyrography

Material:	
Tool burning tip:	
Temperature:	
Shading - 1 firing tip:	
Temperature:	
Shading - 2 firing tip:	
Temperature:	
Shading - 3 firing tip:	
Temperature:	

Settings

Pyrography

Material:	
Tool burning tip:	
Temperature:	
Shading - 1 firing tip:	
Temperature:	
Shading - 2 firing tip:	
Temperature:	
Shading - 3 firing tip:	
Temperature:	

Settings

Pyrography

Material:	
Tool burning tip:	
Temperature:	
Shading - 1 firing tip:	
Temperature:	
Shading - 2 firing tip:	
Temperature:	
Shading - 3 firing tip:	
Temperature:	

Settings

Pyrography

Material:	
Tool burning tip:	
Temperature:	
Shading - 1 firing tip:	
Temperature:	
Shading - 2 firing tip:	
Temperature:	
Shading - 3 firing tip:	
Temperature:	

Settings

Pyrography

Material:	
Tool burning tip:	
Temperature:	
Shading - 1 firing tip:	
Temperature:	
Shading - 2 firing tip:	
Temperature:	
Shading - 3 firing tip:	
Temperature:	

Settings

Pyrography

Material:	
Tool burning tip:	
Temperature:	
Shading - 1 firing tip:	
Temperature:	
Shading - 2 firing tip:	
Temperature:	
Shading - 3 firing tip:	
Temperature:	

Settings

Pyrography

Material:	
Tool burning tip:	
Temperature:	
Shading - 1 firing tip:	
Temperature:	
Shading - 2 firing tip:	
Temperature:	
Shading - 3 firing tip:	
Temperature:	

Settings

Pyrography

Material:	
Tool burning tip:	
Temperature:	
Shading - 1 firing tip:	
Temperature:	
Shading - 2 firing tip:	
Temperature:	
Shading - 3 firing tip:	
Temperature:	

Settings

Pyrography

Material:	
Tool burning tip:	
Temperature:	
Shading - 1 firing tip:	
Temperature:	
Shading - 2 firing tip:	
Temperature:	
Shading - 3 firing tip:	
Temperature:	

Settings

Pyrography

Material:	
Tool burning tip:	
Temperature:	
Shading - 1 firing tip:	
Temperature:	
Shading - 2 firing tip:	
Temperature:	
Shading - 3 firing tip:	
Temperature:	

Settings

Pyrography

Material:	
Tool burning tip:	
Temperature:	
Shading - 1 firing tip:	
Temperature:	
Shading - 2 firing tip:	
Temperature:	
Shading - 3 firing tip:	
Temperature:	

Settings

Pyrography

Material:	
Tool burning tip:	
Temperature:	
Shading - 1 firing tip:	
Temperature:	
Shading - 2 firing tip:	
Temperature:	
Shading - 3 firing tip:	
Temperature:	

Settings

Pyrography

Material:	
Tool burning tip:	
Temperature:	
Shading - 1 firing tip:	
Temperature:	
Shading - 2 firing tip:	
Temperature:	
Shading - 3 firing tip:	
Temperature:	

Settings

Pyrography

Material:	
Tool burning tip:	
Temperature:	
Shading - 1 firing tip:	
Temperature:	
Shading - 2 firing tip:	
Temperature:	
Shading - 3 firing tip:	
Temperature:	

Settings

Pyrography

Material:	
Tool burning tip:	
Temperature:	
Shading - 1 firing tip:	
Temperature:	
Shading - 2 firing tip:	
Temperature:	
Shading - 3 firing tip:	
Temperature:	

Settings

Pyrography

Material:	
Tool burning tip:	
Temperature:	
Shading - 1 firing tip:	
Temperature:	
Shading - 2 firing tip:	
Temperature:	
Shading - 3 firing tip:	
Temperature:	

Settings

Pyrography

Material:	
Tool burning tip:	
Temperature:	
Shading - 1 firing tip:	
Temperature:	
Shading - 2 firing tip:	
Temperature:	
Shading - 3 firing tip:	
Temperature:	

Settings

Pyrography

Material:	
Tool burning tip:	
Temperature:	
Shading - 1 firing tip:	
Temperature:	
Shading - 2 firing tip:	
Temperature:	
Shading - 3 firing tip:	
Temperature:	

Settings

Pyrography

Material:	
Tool burning tip:	
Temperature:	
Shading - 1 firing tip:	
Temperature:	
Shading - 2 firing tip:	
Temperature:	
Shading - 3 firing tip:	
Temperature:	

Amazon item number.: B09ZMVJ7Z6

Woodburning designs and
patterns from the book
in SVG format
free download..

https://bit.ly/3LmC4D1

ISBN: 9798421308225

Impressum

© 2022

Alexander Walter

Habichtshöhe 1b

48282 Emsdetten

USt-IdNr: DE345175172

St.Nr.:   311 5218 2830

Druck: Amazon KDP

Made in United States
Troutdale, OR
02/19/2024

17814659R00071